TALES FRO

In the old days, people did not move around so much. They often lived in the same village all their lives. Everybody knew everybody, knew their parents, their children, their grandparents, and probably knew all their secrets too.

So when John Lackland's son returns to the village of Longpuddle after thirty years in America, he knows he will find many of the same families there. In the town he catches the Longpuddle wagon, and on the way to the village he asks the other passengers for news.

The passengers are very happy to tell him stories. There's a good story about Tony Kytes and all his young women – oh yes, Mr Lackland must hear that one. And what about Andrew and Jane, and the parson and the fox? The postmistress tells Mr Lackland that story, and then the schoolteacher tells him why the church band stopped playing their fiddles in the church twenty years ago. And does Mr Lackland remember Netty Sargent? He does, and so Mrs Pawle, a farmer's wife, tells him what Netty had to do to get her uncle's house . . .

OXFORD BOOKWORMS LIBRARY
Classics

Tales from Longpuddle

Stage 2 (700 headwords)

Series Editor: Jennifer Bassett
Founder Editor: Tricia Hedge
Activities Editors: Jennifer Bassett and Christine Lindop

THOMAS HARDY

Tales from Longpuddle

Retold by
Jennifer Bassett

Illustrated by
Brian Walker

OXFORD UNIVERSITY PRESS

OXFORD
UNIVERSITY PRESS

Great Clarendon Street, Oxford OX2 6DP

Oxford New York

Auckland Bangkok Buenos Aires Cape Town Chennai
Dar es Salaam Delhi Hong Kong Istanbul Karachi Kolkata
Kuala Lumpur Madrid Melbourne Mexico City Mumbai Nairobi
São Paulo Shanghai Taipei Tokyo Toronto

Oxford and Oxford English are registered trade marks
of Oxford University Press in the UK and in certain other countries

ISBN 0 19 422993 9

The four stories in this volume are from Thomas Hardy's
A Few Crusted Characters and in their original versions were
published under the titles *Tony Kytes, the Arch-Deceiver;
Andrey Satchel and the Parson and Clerk;
Absent-Mindedness in a Parish Choir; Netty Sargent's Copyhold*

Printed in Spain by Unigraf s.l.

CONTENTS

The Wagon to Longpuddle

IT IS A SATURDAY afternoon in autumn, in the High Street of a well-known town. A large carrier's wagon stands outside the Town Hall, and the horses wait quietly, eating from their nose-bags. On the side of the wagon, in large yellow letters, are the words, 'BURTHEN, CARRIER TO LONGPUDDLE.'

It is now half-past three by the clock on the Town Hall, and the wagon will leave at four. Slowly, people begin to arrive and take their seats. First, two women climb up, and then a third, who is the postmistress at Longpuddle. At five minutes to four, more people arrive. There is Mr Profitt, the schoolteacher, and Christopher Twink, the builder, with his old father. Then come a farmer and his wife, and last of all, Mr Flaxton, the church clerk.

By now Burthen, the carrier, is getting the horses ready, and soon he climbs up to the driving seat.

'Is everybody here?' he asks the passengers.

The people who are not there do not reply, of course, and a minute or two later the wagon begins to move along the High Street. When it comes to the bridge over the river at the bottom end of the town, the postmistress suddenly calls out to the carrier.

'Mr Burthen,' she says. 'There's a man calling you, over there by the corner. I think he wants you to stop for him.'

Burthen stops the wagon, and waits while the man comes towards them. 'Now who's that, then?' he says. 'That's not a Longpuddle man.'

'I've never seen him before,' says the schoolteacher.

Then the stranger arrives. 'Can you take another passenger for Longpuddle?' he asks.

'We can take one more,' says the carrier. 'Where are you from, sir? You're not from round here, are you?'

'I am,' says the stranger. 'I was born at Longpuddle, and my father and grandfather before me.'

The postmistress is watching him with interest. 'Oh!' she says suddenly. 'I know who you are! You're John Lackland's son – he who went to America thirty years ago with his wife and family.'

'That's right,' says the stranger, smiling. 'John Lackland was my father. And now I've come home to have a look at the old village, and find some old friends. Are the same families still living there?'

'Many of them are,' says the church clerk. 'Which names do you remember?'

'There was a boy called Tony Kytes, I remember.'

2

'Oh yes,' says the clerk. 'Tony Kytes is a married man now. Lives over at Mellstock, I think.'

'And he nearly got married to three women,' laughs the carrier. 'There's a good story about Tony and all his young women.'

'Tell me about it,' says John Lackland's son.

And this is the carrier's story.

'Now who's that then?' says the carrier.
'That's not a Longpuddle man.'

Tony Kytes Finds a Wife

I SHALL NEVER forget Tony's face. It was a little, round face, with bright black eyes. He never smiled very much, but he was a great favourite with the women. And *he* liked *them*, oh yes! One week you saw him walking along with one girl, the next week you saw him with another girl.

But in the end he decided that Milly Richards was the girl for him. She was a nice, sweet little thing, and people soon said they were engaged to be married.

One Saturday Tony went to market, to do some business for his father, and he drove the wagon home in the afternoon. When he got to the hill just outside the town, he saw Unity Sallet by the side of the road. He knew Unity very well. Once, he nearly asked her to marry him – but then he got together with Milly.

When Tony came up to her in the wagon, Unity said, 'My dear Tony, can I ride home with you?'

'Of course you can, my love,' said Tony. 'I couldn't say no to you, could I?'

So Unity smiled, jumped up into the wagon and Tony drove on up the hill.

'Tony,' she said, in a soft little voice, 'why did you leave

'I think you're the prettiest girl in the world,' said Tony.

me for that other girl? How is she better than I am? I'll be a fine wife, and a loving one, too. And you've known me for a long time, haven't you, Tony?'

'Yes, I have,' said Tony. 'Yes, that's very true.'

'And – can you say I'm not pretty, Tony?'

He looked at her for a long while. 'I really can't,' said he. 'No, I think you're the prettiest girl in the world.'

'So I'm prettier than *she* is, am I?'

Luckily, before Tony could answer, he saw a girl's hat over the hedge round a turning in the road. He knew the hat very well – it was Milly's hat.

'Unity,' said Tony quickly, 'here's Milly coming now.

5

I'll be in terrible trouble if she sees you with me. Now, dearest Unity, we don't want any fighting or anything, do we? So will you lie down in the back of the wagon, under the tarpaulin? Just until Milly has passed? And I'll think about what you said, and perhaps I'll put a loving question to you, and not Milly. Nothing is decided yet between her and me, you know.'

So Unity lay down under the tarpaulin in the back of the wagon, and Tony drove on to meet Milly.

'My dear Tony!' Milly said crossly, when he came near. 'How late you are!'

'Late?' said Tony. 'Were you waiting for me?'

'Of course I was!' said Milly. 'You asked me to meet you, to ride home with you. Don't you remember?'

'Oh dear!' said Tony. 'Yes, yes, I did. I remember now. Oh dear – I mean, jump in then, Milly dear!'

So Milly climbed into the wagon and Tony drove on. They talked about this and that, and looked at the trees and the birds. Then they came to a house by the road, and looking out of an upstairs window was Hannah Jolliver. Now Hannah was a tall, good-looking girl, with long red hair. And Tony was in love with her for a long time – before Milly, and before Unity.

'My dear Milly,' he said, in a whisper, because he didn't want Unity to hear, 'there's a young woman looking out of that window, who wanted to marry me. I'm afraid she's going to be angry, because she's found out that I'm going to marry you. And you're a prettier girl than she is. So, Milly, will you help me?'

'Of course, dearest Tony,' said Milly.

'Then will you hide under the empty sacks just here in the front of the wagon, behind the seat? She hasn't seen us yet, and then there won't be any angry words.'

'Well, all right, if it helps you, Tony,' said Milly. She didn't really want to, but she got down behind the seat and hid under the sacks. So there was Milly hiding in the front of the wagon, and Unity hiding in the back.

Tony drove on past the house, which was Hannah's uncle's house, and Hannah looked down from the window and called out to him, 'Aren't you going to ask me to ride home with you?'

'Oh – yes, of course!' said Tony, who didn't know what to say. 'But aren't you staying at your uncle's?'

'No, I'm not,' said Hannah. 'Can't you see I've got my hat and coat on? How can you be so stupid, Tony?'

'Um, yes, um, then you must ride home with me, of course,' said Tony, who was beginning to feel hot and uncomfortable. So he stopped the wagon, while Hannah ran downstairs and got in beside him.

Tony drove on again, and then Hannah looked at him out of the corner of her eye. 'This is nice, isn't it, Tony?' she said. 'I like riding with you.'

Tony looked back into her eyes. 'And I like riding with you,' he said after a while. Then he looked into her eyes again – a good, long, slow look. He began to like her more and more. And then he couldn't remember why he ever wanted to marry Milly or Unity. He moved nearer to

Milly got down behind the seat and hid under the sacks.

8

Hannah on the seat, and they talked in soft little whispers. And after a time Tony said, 'Ah, my sweet Hannah!' and took hold of her hand.

'I'm sorry that you're going to marry Milly,' Hannah said, 'because I do like you very much, Tony dear.'

Tony gave a quick look behind him. 'I haven't asked her the question yet,' he whispered, 'and I'm not sure I will. I'm thinking about asking *you*.'

'Ooooh! Leave Milly, and marry me!' cried Hannah loudly. 'Oh, how wonderful!'

At this, there was a sudden little angry scream from behind the seat, and the tarpaulin at the back moved.

Hannah looked round. 'Something's there, Tony! There's an animal in the back of the wagon!'

'No, no,' said Tony. 'It's just empty sacks, and it's the wheels that make that little screaming sound.'

But he knew that he was in trouble, and he didn't know what to do next. Then the wagon came round a corner in the road and Tony saw his father in a field. His father held up his hand, and Tony saw his escape.

'Oh, Hannah,' he said, 'can you hold the horse for a minute, while I go and find out what father wants?'

Hannah agreed, and Tony hurried into the field.

'What are you playing at, Tony?' said old Mr Kytes.

'What do you mean, father?'

'Well, if you're going to marry Milly Richards, do it. But

don't go driving around the country with Jolliver's daughter. People will talk. You mustn't do it, boy.'

'Milly's there, too, father.'

'Milly? Where?'

'Under the sacks! Yes, and Unity Sallet is in there too, father, at the other end, under the tarpaulin. All three of them are in that wagon, and I don't know what to do! Which one shall I marry, father?'

'All three of them are in that wagon, and I don't know what to do!'

'Which one of them did *not* ask to ride with you?'

'That was Milly, because I asked *her*.'

'Then marry Milly, she's the best— Hey, look!'

Tony looked round, and saw his wagon moving. He began to run across the field as fast as he could.

What was happening in the wagon? Milly, under the sacks, was the one who screamed. She began to move about, and then saw another woman's foot. So she moved along under the tarpaulin until she found Unity.

'And what are you doing here?' she asked angrily.

'I can ask you the same question,' said Unity.

'I'm engaged to be married to him, and I can—'

'Oh no, you're not,' said Unity. 'He's going to have Hannah, not you. He said it just now – we heard him.'

When Hannah heard voices under the tarpaulin, she forgot the horse and turned round. The horse decided to go home, and moved off much too quickly. The wheels of the wagon went up on the side of the field, the wagon turned over, and all three girls fell out into the road. The horse looked round and stood still.

Nobody was hurt, but when Tony ran up, the three girls were all shouting and crying and screaming.

'Oh, don't be angry, my dears! Please don't!' said Tony. They did not stop crying and screaming, so he spoke more loudly. 'I must do what's right,' he said. 'I've asked Hannah to marry me, and she's agreed—'

*When Tony ran up, the girls were all shouting
and crying and screaming.*

'Oh no, I haven't!' said Hannah, really angry now. 'You must think I'm soft in the head! I'm not marrying a man who keeps girls in the back of his wagon!'

Tony looked surprised. 'So you won't marry me, Hannah?' he said.

'Never!' said Hannah, and she walked away. Perhaps she did still want him, but she didn't want to say so in front of the other girls.

Tony didn't know what to say next. Milly was crying her eyes out, and Tony's father thought that she was the best wife for him. But you never do what your father tells you to, do you? So Tony turned to Unity.

'Well, will you marry me, Unity dear?' he said.

'Marry something that Hannah Jolliver doesn't want? Not I!' said Unity. And she walked away too.

So then it was just Milly and Tony. Milly was still crying, and Tony stood there and looked at her.

'Well, here we are,' he said at last. 'Just the two of us. We'll get married then, shall we, Milly?'

'If you like, Tony. You didn't really mean what you said to them?'

'Not a word of it!' said Tony. And then he kissed her, put the wagon back on the road, and they drove home. They went to see the parson the very next Sunday, and were married two Sundays later.

x x x

At the end of his story the carrier turns to the postmistress. 'They had a fine wedding, Mrs Weedle, didn't they? You were there, weren't you?'

'Oh yes,' says the postmistress. 'Best wedding party for years. And I've been to a lot of them. We've had some strange weddings too. Do you remember Andrew Satchel and Jane Vallens a few years ago?'

'But they got married in a different village,' says the church clerk quickly. 'Not in Longpuddle church.'

The carrier laughs. 'It's all right, Mr Flaxton. We know it wasn't you. Go on, Mrs Weedle, tell our visitor about Andrew and Jane.'

'Yes, I remember the Satchel family,' says John Lackland's son. 'I'd like to hear that story.'

And this is the postmistress's story.

Andrew, Jane, the Parson, and the Fox

IT ALL HAPPENED because Andrew Satchel liked his drink too much. Jane Vallens, his bride, was some years older than him, and was in a great hurry to get married. Andrew agreed to marry her because of the baby, but he didn't really want to get married, and Jane, poor thing, was afraid of losing him. She was very anxious to get him to church as soon as possible.

So she was very happy, early on a fine November morning, when she and Andrew walked to the church just outside her village. Andrew's brother and sister went with them, to be their witnesses. After the wedding Andrew and Jane planned to go down to Port Bredy and spend the day there, as a little holiday.

When Andrew left Longpuddle that morning, to walk to his bride's village, people said that he was walking all over the road, first one side, then the other. The night before, you see, he was at his neighbour's house, for a party to welcome a new baby. It was a good party, and Andrew had no sleep, and a lot of strong drink.

He got to the church with Jane, they walked inside, and the parson looked at Andrew very hard.

'What's this? You're drunk, my man! And so early in the morning, too! That's disgraceful!'

'Well, that's true, sir,' said Andrew. 'But I can stand, and I can walk. Better than a lot of people. *You* couldn't stand and walk after a party at Tom Forrest's house, could you, Parson? No, you couldn't!'

This answer didn't please Parson Billy Toogood a bit. He was strong on church business inside the church, but he was very different outside the church, I can tell you.

'I cannot marry you when you are drunk, and I will not!' he said. 'Go home and get sober!'

Then the bride began to cry. 'Oh Parson, please marry us, please!'

'I cannot marry you when you are drunk, and I will not!'
said the parson.

'No, I won't,' said Mr Toogood. 'I won't marry you to a man who is drunk. It's not right. I'm sorry for you, young woman, because I can see that you need to get married, but you must go home. How could you bring him here drunk like this?'

'But if he doesn't come drunk, he won't come at all, sir!' said Jane, still crying hard.

But Parson Toogood still said no.

'Well, sir,' said Jane, 'please will you go home and leave us here for two hours? When you come back, Andrew will be sober. But I want to stay here, because if Andrew goes out of this church unmarried, wild horses won't get him back here again!'

'Very well,' said Parson Toogood. 'I'll give you two hours, and then I'll come back.'

Andrew's brother and sister didn't want to wait all that time, so the church clerk sent them home. 'We'll find some other people to be witnesses,' he said.

Then the bride whispered in the parson's ear. 'Please, sir, will you lock the door – and not tell anyone we are here? And perhaps it will be better if you put us in the church tower. If we stay here in the church, people can look in the windows and see us and talk about it. And perhaps Andrew will try to get out and leave me!'

'All right,' said the parson. 'We'll lock you in.'

Then he and the church clerk went home, the parson

'Perhaps it will be better if you put us in the church tower,'
whispered Jane.

into his house, and the clerk into the garden. The clerk
worked for the parson, you see – in the garden, taking care
of his horses, and that kind of thing. And both of them,
parson and clerk, dearly loved following the hunt.

Well, on that day the hunt was meeting near the
parson's village, and soon both the parson and the clerk

could hear the noise of the horses, and the dogs, and everything. The clerk hurried into the house.

'Sir,' he said. 'The hunt's here, and your horses need a run very badly, sir. They haven't been out for days!'

'You're right,' said Parson Toogood. 'Yes, the horses must go out. Go and get them ready! We'll take them out, just for an hour, and then come back.'

So the clerk got the horses ready, and he and the parson rode off to find the hunt. When they got there, the parson found a lot of friends, and soon they were all talking and laughing together. Then the dogs found a fox, and away they all went – the huntsmen in their red coats, the squire from the big house with his friends, the farmers and their sons, and the parson and the clerk.

He was a great hunting man, was Parson Toogood. He forgot all about the unmarried man and woman locked in his church tower, and so did the clerk.

Across the fields they rode, over the hedges, through the rivers, in and out of woods, up and down the hills. It was a fine, exciting run that day, and the parson and the clerk enjoyed themselves very much. At one time the fox turned back, and ran right under the nose of Parson Toogood's horse.

'Halloo! Halloo!' shouted the parson. 'There he goes!' and away they all went again.

At last, late in the day, the hunt came to an end. The

'Halloo! Halloo!' shouted the parson. 'There he goes!'

parson and the clerk were a long way from home, and their horses were tired. They rode home very slowly.

'Oh dear, my back does hurt!' said Parson Toogood.

'I can't keep my eyes open,' said the clerk. 'I'm so tired!'

It was dark when they got home. They made the horses comfortable, ate something, and fell into bed themselves.

The next morning, when Parson Toogood was having breakfast, the clerk came running in through the door.

'Oh sir!' he cried. 'Those two in the church tower – we forgot all about them! They'll still be there!'

Parson Toogood jumped up from his chair. 'Oh dear!' he said. 'Oh dear, oh dear! This is disgraceful!'

'It is, sir; very. And that poor woman . . .'

'Don't say it, clerk! If she's had the baby, and no doctor or nurse with her . . . Come on!'

So they both ran round to the church, looked up at the tower, and saw a little white face looking down at them. It was the bride.

'They're still there,' said the parson. He turned his face away. 'Oh dear, oh dear! What *am* I going to say to them? Is she all right, clerk? Can you see?'

'I don't know, sir. I can't see lower than her neck.'

'Well, how does her face look?'

'White, sir. Very, very white.'

'Well, we must go in and see them. Oh dear, oh dear! And my back still hurts from that ride yesterday!'

*The parson and the clerk saw a little white face
looking down at them.*

They went into the church and unlocked the tower door,
and at once poor Jane and Andrew jumped out like hungry
cats from a cupboard. Andrew was very sober now, and his
bride was white in the face, but all right in other ways.

'Thank God for that!' said Parson Toogood. 'But why
didn't you try to escape? Why didn't you shout from the top
of the tower, to get help?'

22

'She didn't want me to,' said Andrew.

Jane began to cry again. 'It was the disgrace of it,' she said. 'We thought people would talk about it and laugh at us all our lives. So we waited and waited and waited – but you never came back, parson!'

'Yes, I'm sorry about that,' said Parson Toogood. 'Very sorry. But now, let's get on with the wedding.'

'I'd like something to eat first,' said Andrew. 'Just a piece of bread. I'm so hungry – I could eat a horse!'

'Oh, let's get married first,' said the bride anxiously, 'while the parson's still here. It won't take a minute.'

'Oh, all right,' said Andrew.

The clerk was one witness, and he called in a second witness (telling him not to talk about it). Very soon Andrew and Jane were husband and wife.

'Now,' said Parson Toogood, 'you two must come back to my house and eat a good meal.'

So they went back with the parson, and ate nearly every bit of food in his house.

They kept the secret for a while, but then the story got out, and everybody knew about their night in the church tower. Even Andrew and Jane laugh about it now. Andrew isn't much of a husband, it's true, but Jane got a ring on her finger and a name for her baby.

x x x

23

The carrier laughs loudly at the end of the postmistress's story. 'Did you know Andrew's uncle?' he asks John Lackland's son. 'He played in the church band.'

'The church band!' says Mr Lackland. 'Are they still playing their fiddles in the church every Sunday?'

'No,' says Mr Profitt, the schoolteacher. 'They haven't played for twenty years or more. There's an organ in the church now. The young man who plays it is very good, but most people liked the fiddles better. Yes, everybody in Longpuddle was sorry when the church band stopped playing.'

'But why did they stop,' says John Lackland's son, 'if everybody liked them?'

And this is what the schoolteacher tells him.

The Church Band

IT WAS ON the Sunday after Christmas. That was the last time the band played in Longpuddle church, but they didn't know it at the time, of course.

They were a very good band, the best of all the villages around. There was Nicholas Puddingcome, who played the first fiddle. There was Timothy Thomas and John Biles on the other fiddles; and Dan Hornhead and Robert Dowdle played the oboes.

They didn't just play church music; they could play all kinds of dance music too. They often went out to play at dancing parties in people's homes or in the village inn. So one night they were in the squire's big house, playing nice Christmas songs, and drinking tea with all the squire's fine friends. And the next night they were down at the Dog and Fox, playing noisy dance music for twenty dancers, and drinking hot brandy-and-water.

Well, that Christmas week was a busy time for them. They were out at dance parties every night, and got very little sleep. Then came the Sunday after Christmas. It was cold that winter – oh my word, it was cold! And upstairs in the church gallery, it was even colder.

The band slept like babies all through the sermon.

So when the band was playing on that Sunday morning, Nicholas Puddingcome said to the others:

'I can't feel my fingers, it's so cold. How can a man play the fiddle when he can't feel his fingers? This afternoon we'll have something to make us warm.'

So he brought a big jar of hot brandy-and-water to church in the afternoon. They put the jar inside Timothy

Thomas's fiddle bag, which kept it nice and warm. And during that long afternoon in church, they all had a little glass now and then, so when the parson began his sermon, they were all feeling comfortable and warm. Unluckily for them, the sermon that day was a long one, and the parson went on and on and on. And every man in the band fell asleep, and they slept like babies all through the sermon.

It was a very dark afternoon, and by the end of the sermon you couldn't see very much inside the church. When the parson finished, he called for the last piece of music. But the band did not start playing, and people began to turn round and look up at the gallery. Then Levi Limpet, a boy who sat in the gallery, whispered to Nicholas, 'Begin! Begin!'

'Hey? What?' said Nicholas, and nearly fell out of his chair.

Then, because the church was dark and he was still half-asleep, he thought that he was at a party. The night before, you see, the band was playing all night at a party at the Dog and Fox, and Nicholas thought he was still there! So he took his fiddle and immediately began to play *The Laughing Sailor* – that was the favourite dance tune in our village that winter.

The rest of the band woke up suddenly, and hearing *The Laughing Sailor*, of course they just followed Nicholas. And away they all went, fiddles and oboes, as loudly as they could. They played that dance tune until the church walls shook with the sound.

Then Nicholas saw that nobody was moving. If people didn't know the dances, he often called out the moves to help them. And so he did that now.

'Up to the top, change hands, then back down the other side!' he shouted. 'Then turn around, once, twice, take hands, and back to the top again!'

The boy Levi was very frightened. He ran down the gallery stairs and out of the church as fast as his little legs could carry him. The parson's hair stood on end when he heard that wicked dance tune in his church. He held up his hand and cried, 'Stop, stop, stop! Stop, stop!'

But the band didn't hear him because of the noise of the music. The parson went on calling 'Stop, stop!' and the band went on playing.

Then people in the church began to stand up and talk. 'What's happening? Why are they playing this wicked music? Is it the Devil himself up there in the gallery?'

And the squire, too, stood up. He was there with all his fine friends, and he was very angry. He went and stood in front of the gallery, and shouted at the band.

'Stop this wicked noise! At once! D'you hear?'

The squire had a good, loud voice, and at last the band heard him, and stopped playing.

'Playing the Devil's music in church – in God's house!'

'Stop this wicked noise! At once! D'you hear?'

said the squire. 'I have never heard anything so disgraceful in all my life – never!' Oh, he was so angry!

The parson came down and stood beside the squire. 'Never!' he said. 'Never!'

'The Devil is in you men!' said the squire. (He was a wicked man himself, the squire was, but that day he was all on God's side, of course.) 'And you will *never*,' the squire went on, '*never, never* play your fiddles in this church again! You have done a wicked thing today, and it must never happen again.'

By now the unhappy players knew that they were in church, and not in the Dog and Fox. They put their fiddles and their oboes under their arms, and very quietly they went down the gallery stairs and out of the back door of the church.

The parson was a kind man, and when he heard the true story later, he wasn't angry any more. He knew that Nicholas, Timothy and the rest weren't wicked men. But the squire – that was a different matter. He was a hard man, and when he said 'no more fiddles', he meant 'no more fiddles'. He sent away for an organ, and the next week, there it was in the church. He found a young man from a good family to play it, and the old band played no more in Longpuddle church.

✗ ✗ ✗

*Very quietly the band went down the gallery stairs
and out of the church.*

After this story John Lackland's son asks about the young women of the village. 'Or those who were young when I left, all those years ago,' he says. 'They're all married now, I'm sure.'

'Let's see,' says the carrier. 'Do you remember Netty Sargent, sir?'

'Netty Sargent . . . Yes, I do. When I left, she was living with her uncle, wasn't she?'

'That's right. She was a bright young thing, Netty was. Nothing bad about her, you understand, just a little bit clever. She was very clever about the leasehold of her house, I remember.' The carrier looks round at his passengers. 'Who'll tell Mr Lackland that story, then?'

'My wife knew Netty when they were girls,' says the farmer, Mr Pawle. 'She can tell you.'

Nancy Pawle is a big, comfortable-looking woman. She laughs, and says, 'Oh yes, I can tell you all about Netty Sargent.'

Netty Sargent and the House

NETTY SARGENT lived with her uncle in that lonely house just outside the grounds of the squire's big house. She was a tall young woman, with black hair and dancing eyes. And she had a little laughing smile that sent all the young men wild.

All the young men of that time were after her, but in the end she decided that Jasper Cliff was her favourite. He was good-looking, but he only ever thought about himself, not other people. But Netty wanted Jasper, and none of the others. Jasper liked Netty too, but he was more interested in her uncle's house.

The house was built by Netty's great-great-grandfather, and had a garden and a little field next to it. But it was a leasehold house, because the ground belonged to the squire.

'And what happens,' Jasper asked Netty one day, 'when your uncle dies?'

'The house, garden and field will go back to the squire,' said Netty. 'But if Uncle pays a few pounds, he can renew the leasehold and put another name on it. Then the squire can't get the house back until that person dies.'

'And what is your uncle going to do?' asked Jasper.

33

'Oh, he's going to renew the leasehold, and put my name on it. He told me that months ago.'

Netty's uncle knew that it was important to renew the leasehold, because the squire was very anxious to get the house back. The squire didn't like all those little leaseholds on his ground, and he wanted to pull the house down and make it all nice and tidy.

Netty's uncle knew this very well – but he still didn't renew the leasehold. He didn't like Jasper Cliff, so perhaps he didn't like to think of Jasper marrying Netty and living in the house when he was dead.

Every week Jasper asked Netty about the leasehold, and Netty asked her uncle, and her uncle said, 'I'll go and see the squire's agent next week.' But still nothing happened.

At last old Mr Sargent fell ill, and Jasper got tired of waiting. 'Why doesn't your uncle do it?' he asked Netty. 'I tell you, if you lose the house and ground, I won't marry you. And there's an end of it.'

Poor Netty hurried indoors to talk to her uncle.

'Please do something, Uncle!' she said. 'If I don't get the house, I won't get a husband!'

'And you must have Jasper, must you, my dear?'

'Yes, Uncle, I must!'

Old Sargent didn't want to make Netty unhappy, so he asked for a meeting with the squire's agent. The squire was very cross when he heard this. He was hoping that old

'If you lose the house and ground,' said Jasper,
'I won't marry you.'

Sargent would die and the leasehold would come to an end.
But he had to agree to renew the leasehold if Sargent paid
the money. So the squire's agent got the new papers ready
for old Sargent to sign.

By now Netty's uncle was really ill, and couldn't leave
the house. The agent agreed to visit him. 'I'll come at five
o'clock on Monday,' he told Netty, 'and Mr Sargent can
pay the money and sign the papers then.'

35

At three o'clock on that Monday Netty brought her uncle a cup of tea. When she came in the room, her uncle gave a little cry and fell forward in his chair. Netty ran to him, but he could not speak or move. And in a few minutes, she saw that his face and hands were cold and white. He was dead, stone-cold dead.

Netty was very unhappy. 'Why didn't he live two more hours?' she thought. 'Now I've lost everything – house, garden, field, and a home for myself and my lover. What *am* I going to do now?'

Then, suddenly, she knew what she had to do. It was a dark December afternoon, which was very helpful for her. First, she locked the front door. Then she moved her uncle's table in front of the fire. Her uncle's body was still in his chair, which was a big old chair on wheels. So she pushed the chair, with her uncle in it, to the table, putting the chair with its back half-turned to the window.

On the table she put the large family Bible open in front of him, and put his finger on the page. Then she opened his eyes a little, and put his glasses on his nose. When it got dark, she lit a candle and put it on the table beside the Bible. Then she unlocked the door, and sat down to wait.

When she heard the agent's knock at five o'clock, she hurried to the door.

'I'm sorry, sir,' she whispered. 'Uncle's so ill tonight. I'm afraid he can't see you.'

The agent was not very pleased. 'So I've come out all this way for nothing, have I?'

'Oh no, sir, I hope not,' said Netty. 'We can do the business about the leasehold, can't we?'

'Of course not. He must pay the money, and sign the leasehold papers in front of me. I have to be a witness.'

Netty looked worried. 'Uncle is so afraid of business things like this. His hands were shaking when I told him that you were coming today.'

'Poor old man – I'm sorry for him,' said the agent. 'But he must sign the papers, and I must be a witness.'

'Yes, I understand that, sir,' said Netty. She thought for a minute. 'You have to see *him*. But can you still be a witness, sir, if *he* doesn't see *you*?'

'How do you mean, girl?' said the agent.

'Come with me a minute,' she said.

She took him into the garden and round to the window. Inside, the agent could see, at the other end of the room, the back and side of the old man's head, and his arm. He could see the glasses on his nose, and the book and the candle on the table.

'He's reading his Bible, sir,' said Netty, in her softest, sweetest voice.

'Yes, I see that,' said the agent. 'But nobody ever sees him in church, do they?'

'No, but he loves his Bible,' said Netty. 'I think he's

sleeping a little at the moment, but that's not surprising in
an old man, who's so unwell. Now, sir, can you stand here
at the window and watch him sign the papers? Then he
won't see you, and he won't be worried and unhappy about
it all. Can you do that for him, sir?'

'Very well,' said the agent. He took out a cigar, lit it, and
began to smoke. 'Have you got the money ready?'

'Can you stand here at the window and watch him
sign the papers?' said Netty.

'Yes,' said Netty. 'I'll bring it out.' She hurried inside, and brought out the money. The agent counted it, then gave Netty the leasehold papers.

'Uncle's hand is very shaky now,' she said. 'And he's so sleepy. I don't think he signs his name very well.'

'He doesn't have to have beautiful writing. He just has to sign,' said the agent.

'Can I hold his hand, to help him?'

'Yes, hold his hand, girl – that'll be all right.'

Netty went into the house, and the agent went on smoking his cigar outside the window. He saw Netty put the pen and the papers in front of her uncle, and touch his arm, and speak to him. She showed him where to write his name on the papers, and put the pen in his hand. Then she stood behind him, and held his hand. But the agent could still see a bit of his head, and he saw the old man's hand write his name on the papers.

Then Netty came out and gave the papers to the agent, and the agent signed his name as witness. He gave her the paper signed by the squire, and left.

And the next morning Netty told the neighbours that her uncle was dead in his bed.

So that's how Netty Sargent lost her house and field, and got them back again – with a husband. But Jasper was a mistake as a husband. After a few years he started hitting Netty – not very hard, but it made her angry. Then she told

The agent saw the old man's hand write his name on the papers.

a neighbour about the leasehold business, and the story got around. By then the old squire was dead, and the squire's son got to hear the story. But Netty was a pretty young woman, and the squire's son never did anything about it.

x x x

Soon the carrier's wagon came down the hill into Longpuddle, and everybody got out and went home. John Lackland's son went to find a room at the Dog and Fox. He stayed in Longpuddle for a few days, walking around, looking at things, and talking to people. Then he left, and no one saw him again.

'Where did he go?' the schoolteacher asked Mrs Weedle in the post office one day.

'I don't know,' said Mrs Weedle. 'He didn't tell anyone. He just went.'

'Why did he come back to Longpuddle, do you think?'

'He said he just wanted to see the place where he was a child. But perhaps he came back to get a wife, and couldn't find one. Who knows?'

GLOSSARY

agent somebody who does business for another person

anxious worried and afraid; if you are anxious to do something,
   you want to do it very much

band a group of people who play music together

Bible the holy book of the Christian church

brandy a strong alcoholic drink

bride a woman on the day of her wedding

candle a stick of wax that burns to give light

care, take care of to do for somebody the things that they need

clerk somebody who helps a parson in his work for the church

Devil the opposite of God

disgrace *(adj* **disgraceful)** when other people stop thinking well
   of you, because you have done something very bad

drunk behaving differently because of drinking too much
   alcohol

engaged when you have agreed to marry somebody

farmer somebody who keeps animals and grows food to sell

fiddle *(n)* a musical instrument with strings (a violin)

fox a wild animal, like a dog, with a long tail and red fur

gallery in a church, a place upstairs where you can sit and look
   down into the church

God the 'person' who made the world and controls all things;
   thank God people say this when they are happy because
   something bad did not happen

hedge a line of small trees that makes a kind of 'wall'

hunt *(n)* when people ride horses and chase foxes with dogs

inn an old word for a pub or hotel, where people go to drink

jar a large container for drink

kiss *(v)* to touch someone lovingly with your lips

leasehold when somebody can use a house or land for a certain time, often many years, before the owner can take it back

neighbour a person who lives near you

oboe a musical instrument, a kind of 'pipe' you blow through

organ a big musical instrument, like a piano with pipes

parson an old word for a priest in the church

postmistress a woman who is in charge of a post office

pretty nice to look at

renew to begin something again, e.g. a leasehold for another period of time

sack a large strong bag for carrying heavy things

sermon a talk that a parson gives in church

sign *(v)* to write your name on a letter, important papers, etc.

sober not drunk

squire (in the past in England) an important man who owned a lot of land in and around a village

stranger a person that you do not know

tarpaulin a heavy sheet, used to cover things to keep rain off

tower a tall part of a building, e.g. on a church

tune musical notes that sound nice when played together (e.g. a song has words and a tune)

uncle the brother of your mother or father

wagon a kind of small open 'car' pulled by a horse or horses

wedding the time when a man and a woman get married

whisper *(v & n)* to speak in a very soft, quiet voice

wicked very bad

witness a person who watches when an important paper is signed, and who also signs the paper

Before Reading

1 Read the story introduction on the first page of the book, and the back cover. How much do you know now about the stories? Tick one box for each sentence.

	YES	NO
1 John Lackland's son was born in Longpuddle.	☐	☐
2 He has lived in Longpuddle all his life.	☐	☐
3 The passengers on the wagon tell him stories about Longpuddle families.	☐	☐
4 Tony Kytes is a clever young man.	☐	☐
5 Tony Kytes is married.	☐	☐
6 All the girls like Tony Kytes.	☐	☐
7 The church band still play their fiddles in church.	☐	☐
8 Netty Sargent wanted her uncle's house.	☐	☐
9 One of the stories has an animal in it.	☐	☐

2 What is going to happen in these stories? Can you guess? Choose answers to complete these sentences. (You can choose more than one answer if you like.)

1 Tony Kytes . . .

a) asks more than one girl to marry him.

b) decides not to marry any of his girlfriends.

c) is in big trouble with all his girlfriends.

d) leaves home and goes to America.

2 In the story about Andrew and Jane . . .

    a) a fox comes into the church during their wedding.

    b) a fox eats their chickens while they are at church.

    c) Andrew shoots a fox in the parson's garden.

    d) the parson goes fox-hunting on their wedding day.

3 The church band stop playing their fiddles in church . . .

    a) because nobody likes their music.

    b) because they play the wrong music one day.

    c) because they play very badly.

    d) because it's too cold in the church.

4 To get her uncle's house, Netty Sargent . . .

    a) had to marry an old man.

    b) didn't tell the truth.

    c) used a dead body to help her.

    d) was very unkind to her brothers and sisters.

3 **You will find some of these things or people in the stories. Can you guess which ones? Tick some boxes.**

☐ cars	☐ guitars	☐ a parson	☐ a footballer
☐ wagons	☐ fiddles	☐ a doctor	☐ a murderer
☐ trains	☐ pianos	☐ a teacher	☐ a farmer
☐ horses	☐ factories	☐ a nurse	☐ a bride
☐ oboes	☐ bicycles	☐ a detective	☐ telephones

While Reading

Read *The Wagon to Longpuddle* and *Tony Kytes Finds a Wife*. Then complete this passage with the right names.

When _____ was driving home from market, he gave _____ a ride in his wagon. Then he saw _____ in the road, and so he asked _____ to hide in the back of the wagon. _____ got into the wagon, but very soon _____ saw _____ looking out of a window. He told _____ that _____ wanted to marry him, and he asked _____ to hide under the sacks in the front of the wagon. When _____ got in, _____ had three girls in his wagon. He went to ask his father what to do, and left _____ holding the horse. But _____ saw _____'s foot under the tarpaulin and spoke to her. _____ heard voices, and then the horse moved off and turned the wagon over. In the end _____ asked all three girls to marry him – first _____, then _____, then _____, but only _____ said yes.

Read *Andrew, Jane, the Parson, and the Fox* to the bottom of page 19. Can you guess how the story ends? Choose answers to these questions.

1 When does the parson remember Andrew and Jane?
   a) That evening
   c) The next day
   b) In the night
   d) Two days later

2 What do Andrew and Jane do during the day?
  a) Call for help   c) Have a fight
  b) Climb out and go home   d) Just wait
3 When do Andrew and Jane get married?
  a) That evening   c) The next week
  b) The next day   d) Never

Read *The Church Band*, and then put these halves of sentences together.

1 The band drank hot brandy-and-water . . .
2 They didn't hear when the sermon finished . . .
3 When they woke up, they began to play dance music . . .
4 The squire bought an organ for the church . . .
5 because they thought they were still in the Dog and Fox.
6 because they were all sleeping like babies.
7 because he didn't want those wicked men to play their fiddles in church ever again.
8 because it was so cold in the church.

Read *Netty Sargent and the House*. Who said these words, and who were they talking to?

1 'The house, garden and field will go back to the squire.'
2 'If you lose the house and ground, I won't marry you.'
3 'And you must have Jasper, must you, my dear?'
4 'Can you still be a witness, . . . if *he* doesn't see *you*?'
5 'Yes, hold his hand, . . . – that'll be all right.'

After Reading

1 Here are some Longpuddle villagers talking. Who are they talking about? Complete the passages with the words below (one word for each gap).

agent, bride, clever, dead, held, hunt, husband, leasehold, like, locked, married, remember, same, signed, three, uncle, until, when, window, witness

1 '. . . So she asked the _____, who had to be the _____, to stand outside the _____. Then she took the _____ papers into the room, put them in front of her _____, spoke to him, and _____ his hand while he _____ his name. And all the time the old man was _____!'

2 'No, he hasn't been out with the _____ for a long time. And I know why! He still feels bad about that time _____ he left a young man and his _____ in the church all night. They were _____ in the tower, and he didn't _____ them _____ the next day.'

3 'Yes, they're getting _____ next Sunday. I don't know if he'll be a good _____ or not. All the girls _____ him, but he's not very _____. Somebody told me that he once asked _____ girls to marry him on the _____ day!'

2 Here is a new illustration for one of the stories. Find the best place for it, and answer these questions.

The picture goes on page _____, in the story _____.

1 Who are these two people?

2 What is the man near the door saying?

3 Why are they both very worried?

Now write a caption for the illustration.

Caption: _____

3 **What did Nicholas say to the parson about the music, later that day? Put their conversation in the right order, and write in the speakers' names. Nicholas speaks first (number 3).**

1 _____ 'Yes, it was. We weren't doing anything wicked.'

2 _____ 'We're going to have an organ. The squire has already sent away for it, and it'll be here by Friday.'

3 _____ 'It was like this, Parson. When we woke up, it—'

4 _____ 'But you were in church, not in the Dog and Fox!'

5 _____ 'Thank you, Parson! So can we play next Sunday?'

6 _____ 'And was that why you played dance music?'

7 _____ 'It was only a little sleep. We were tired, you see, because of playing last night in the Dog and Fox.'

8 _____ 'I'm afraid not. The squire said no more fiddles.'

9 _____ 'Yes, I know, but it was dark, we were half asleep, and we thought we were still at the dance!'

10 _____ 'Woke up? You were asleep during my sermon?'

11 _____ 'But who will play the music in church then?'

12 _____ 'I know you're not a wicked man, Nicholas. Nor are the others. All right, we'll say no more about it.'

Which part of the story did Nicholas *not* tell the parson?

4 **What did Andrew and Jane say in the church tower? Finish Jane's words for her. (Use as many words as you like.)**

ANDREW: It's nearly dark. What are we going to do, Jane?
JANE: We're going to _____.

ANDREW: But I'm hungry. We can't wait for him all night!

JANE: I'm sure _____.

ANDREW: Well, I think he's forgotten us. I'll go up and shout from the top of the tower, to get help.

JANE: _____.

ANDREW: Why not?

JANE: Because of the disgrace. Everybody _____.

ANDREW: Oh. Yes, they will, won't they? We'll just have to sit and wait then.

5 Here are some new titles for the stories. Which titles go with which stories? Which titles do you like best? Why?

A Night in the Tower	Dreaming of the Dog and Fox
A Wagon Full of Girls	Witness at the Window
The Leasehold Wedding	When the Fiddles had to Stop
A Dead Man's Hand	Engaged three Times
Milly Gets Her Man	A Dance Tune for the Squire
An Anxious Bride	The Call of the Hunt

6 What did you think about these stories? Choose some of the characters and complete these sentences.

1 I felt sorry for _____ because _____.
2 I thought _____ was *clever/stupid* when _____.
3 I thought _____ did a *good/bad* thing when _____.
4 I thought _____ was *right/wrong* to _____.
5 I liked it when _____.

51

ABOUT THE AUTHOR

Thomas Hardy (1840–1928) was born in the village of Higher Bockhampton in Dorset, in the south of England. When he was a young man, he often played the fiddle at weddings and parties, and he loved listening to old people telling stories of country life. Were the stories true? Hardy once described one of the old musicians from his village as 'a man who speaks neither truth or lies, but something halfway between the two which is very enjoyable'. Later in his life, Hardy put many of the characters and events from these old tales into his own short stories and novels.

At twenty-two he went to London to work as an architect, and there he started writing poems and stories and novels. His fourth novel, *Far from the Madding Crowd* (1874), was very popular, and from this he earned enough money to stop working and also to get married. Other successful novels followed, but when *Tess of the d'Urbervilles* and *Jude the Obscure* were published, readers did not like them at all, saying they were dark and cruel. After this, Hardy stopped writing novels and returned to poetry.

For most of his life he lived in Dorset with his first wife Emma, and soon after she died he married again. After his death his heart was buried in Emma's grave.

The four tales in this book come from *Life's Little Ironies* (1894), and are part of a group of stories called *A Few Crusted Characters*. Many of Hardy's great novels are dark and sad, but these stories show the lighter side of country life, full of fun and laughter and wicked old squires.

ABOUT BOOKWORMS

OXFORD BOOKWORMS LIBRARY
Classics • True Stories • Fantasy & Horror • Human Interest
Crime & Mystery • Thriller & Adventure

The OXFORD BOOKWORMS LIBRARY offers a wide range of original and adapted stories, both classic and modern, which take learners from elementary to advanced level through six carefully graded language stages:

Stage 1 (400 headwords)	**Stage 4** (1400 headwords)
Stage 2 (700 headwords)	**Stage 5** (1800 headwords)
Stage 3 (1000 headwords)	**Stage 6** (2500 headwords)

More than sixty titles are also available on cassette, and there are many titles at Stages 1 to 4 which are specially recommended for younger learners. In addition to the introductions and activities in each Bookworm, resource material includes photocopiable test worksheets and Teacher's Handbooks, which contain advice on running a class library and using cassettes, and the answers for the activities in the books.

Several other series are linked to the OXFORD BOOKWORMS LIBRARY. They range from highly illustrated readers for young learners, to playscripts, non-fiction readers, and unsimplified texts for advanced learners.

Oxford Bookworms Starters	*Oxford Bookworms Factfiles*
Oxford Bookworms Playscripts	*Oxford Bookworms Collection*

Details of these series and a full list of all titles in the OXFORD BOOKWORMS LIBRARY can be found in *Oxford English* catalogues and also on our website www.oup.com/elt. A selection of titles from the OXFORD BOOKWORMS LIBRARY can be found on the next pages.

The Canterville Ghost

OSCAR WILDE

Retold by John Escott

There has been a ghost in the house for three hundred years, and Lord Canterville's family have had enough of it. So Lord Canterville sells his grand old house to an American family. Mr Hiram B. Otis is happy to buy the house *and* the ghost – because of course Americans don't believe in ghosts.

The Canterville ghost has great plans to frighten the life out of the Otis family. But Americans don't frighten easily – especially not two noisy little boys – and the poor ghost has a few surprises waiting for him.

Huckleberry Finn

MARK TWAIN

Retold by Diane Mowat

Who wants to live in a house, wear clean clothes, be good, and go to school every day? Not young Huckleberry Finn, that's for sure.

So Huck runs away, and is soon floating down the great Mississippi River on a raft. With him is Jim, a black slave who is also running away. But life is not always easy for the two friends.

And there's 300 dollars waiting for anyone who catches poor Jim . . .

New Yorkers

O. HENRY

Retold by Diane Mowat

A housewife, a tramp, a lawyer, a waitress, an actress – ordinary people living ordinary lives in New York in the early 1900s. The city has changed greatly since that time, but its people are much the same. Some are rich, some are poor, some are happy, some are sad, some have found love, some are looking for love.

O. Henry's famous short stories – sensitive, funny, sympathetic – give us vivid pictures of the everyday lives of these New Yorkers.

Stories from the Five Towns

ARNOLD BENNETT

Retold by Nick Bullard

Arnold Bennett is famous for his stories about the Five Towns and the people who live there. They look and sound just like other people, and, like all of us, sometimes they do some very strange things. There's Sir Jee, who is a rich businessman. So why is he making a plan with a burglar? Then there is Toby Hall. Why does he decide to visit Number 11 Child Row, and who does he find there? And then there are the Hessian brothers and Annie Emery – and the little problem of twelve thousand pounds.

The Murders in the Rue Morgue

EDGAR ALLAN POE

Retold by Jennifer Bassett

The room was on the fourth floor, and the door was locked – with the key on the inside. The windows were closed and fastened – on the inside. The chimney was too narrow for a cat to get through. So how did the murderer escape? And whose were the two angry voices heard by the neighbours as they ran up the stairs? Nobody in Paris could find any answers to this mystery.

Except Auguste Dupin, who could see further and think more clearly than other people. The answers to the mystery were all there, but only a clever man could see them.

The Three Strangers and Other Stories

THOMAS HARDY

Retold by Clare West

On a stormy winter night, a stranger knocks at the door of a shepherd's cottage. He is cold and hungry, and wants to get out of the rain. He is welcomed inside, but he does not give his name or his business. Who is he, and where has he come from? And he is only the first visitor to call at the cottage that night . . .

In these three short stories, Thomas Hardy gives us pictures of the lives of shepherds and hangmen, dukes and teachers. But rich or poor, young or old, they all have the same feelings of fear, hope, love, jealousy . . .